AF225034

Leaving the Light On

M.J. Finn

Copyright © 2022

All Rights Reserved

Table of Contents

Dedication

To my sister, who fights hard every day to keep her sobriety as her number one priority. I'm so incredibly proud of how far you've come and I'm looking forward to creating new memories in our future! I love that I no longer carry the burden of your addiction on my shoulders. Thank you for giving me a chance to heal. I know the road to where you are today is anything but easy, but you beat the odds and I'm so proud of you! You're stronger than you give yourself credit for! I thank God every day for bringing you and all of us through your addiction. I will always fight for you!

Acknowledgements

This book tells our raw truth and I wouldn't be here on the other side without my mom and sister believing in one another through all the trials we faced. Here's to each of you for remaining hopeful even during hopeless situations. We could have given up on one another and fallen into a life of victim mentality. For my mom and sister, for believing in the love, we once shared before the darkness hit our family so hard. We stuck together thru trial and error and were able to overcome death and loss and addiction, leading us to healthier lives. Without all of our grit and determination, honesty, and support, this book wouldn't be what it is today for the readers and me. A special thanks to you, my editing team and my project manager Solomon Elias who helped guide me with the book I wanted to share, keeping my true authentic style. Another thank you to my friends and family for giving honest feedback and helping guide me through my author journey. To my sister, who allowed me to tell her raw and emotional story of addiction and her brave partner for giving me his different perspective too. They were vital in the process of writing this book.

About the Author

M.J. Finn is a Georgia native who grew up in the suburbs outside of Atlanta. Now she lives in the mountains of Northwest Georgia with her family. She enjoys camping, kayaking, boating, gardening and cooking. Through meditation and spending time in nature, she has found healing in writing.

Chapter 1: The Epidemic

It's often said that addiction is a family disease. It's more than a family disease, it's a global crisis. So little is being done to turn people's lives around when they find themselves in an impossible fight of their lives in addiction. Many start out simply being prescribed pain medicine after a surgery or injury. Some young adults are handed a pill at a party and not thinking much about it, they swallow to fit in with the crowd. Pain is hard to live with, and to many, it's unbearable, so pain pills are their lifeline to make it through that pain. Most pain medicines are very addictive and often numb someone just enough to get by with daily tasks. The problem arises when they take medicine and their bodies build a tolerance. They need more just to get the same effects. So, they take more than prescribed. Now they can't get it refilled when it runs out because they can't overtake it per medical advice. So, they try whatever they can get their hands on to numb the pain. The opioid epidemic is what I'm referring to, and too many people are falling victim to this. Before that person realizes their brains have been tricked into thinking they must have this medicine to survive. It's more than a want. This person has now crossed the boundary of addiction. That boundary of taking prescription medicine and crossing into drug use happens way more than anyone is talking about. Opioids aren't readily available and require a doctor's prescription and sometimes even a pain management doctor. They are a narcotic and the government has control over who gets them and how much they are given. That's right, a prescribed narcotic. If we got pulled over with narcotics in our car, we would go to jail. But, if the government hands them to you in a bottle with your name on it, you are safe. I'm talking about a pill so strong it can make you appear zombie-like if overtaken. This is what happened to my sister at the age of just fourteen. What started as a way to fit in with her peers by taking Xanax at parties quickly became a problem our entire family would deal with for most of her life. It numbed her just enough not to have to feel the pain in her heart after our dad passed away unexpectedly. Those feelings were a lot for a teen to deal with. She wasn't receiving the counseling to help guide her through those feelings, so like many kids in a difficult situation, she fell into the pit of addiction. At fourteen, her group of friends was mostly cheerleaders and football players. She'd hang out on weekends with the popular crowd. First, the alcohol was passed around like water, and the pills were passed out too. To fit in, you couldn't say no. So, she hid behind the beautiful face and Abercrombie clothes & pretended to be just hanging out with innocent friends. As her older sister, I knew more was happening at these friends' houses. I'd overheard them chatting and plotting what they would do on the weekends together. But I wasn't into the same scene, so I turned a blind eye. The last thing she wanted to hear was her older sister, who was anything but cool giving her a lecture on who she should hang out with. So, I stayed in my lane. I never realized the impact this would have on her life until our family experienced life-changing trauma. It sent her into a spiral of fighting for her life. It consumed her life and all of our lives for the next nineteen years.

Chapter 2: The Blame

The night our lives changed. December 25th, 2002. I was invited to Christmas Eve at my boyfriend's family's house that year. I was twenty years old and had spent every Christmas morning at my own family's home. However, I felt the right thing to do was to split time between our parents' homes, so I said yes. As I left my own family's Christmas gathering at my aunt's house, I said goodbye to my parents last. They pleaded, "Please don't go, Macy," but I said I had to stick to my commitment. My dad joked with a pouty lip, and I went and gave them both a hug goodbye. I drove for over an hour and arrived later in the evening at my boyfriend's parents. Shortly after, everyone headed to bed. As I lay there on the sofa, I couldn't stop the thought of wanting to be at home the next morning. Surely my family would miss me. The tug in my heart wouldn't stop. This just didn't feel right, and I didn't know why. So, I snuck down the hallway and told my boyfriend I was going to drive back home. He asked me not to, but I told him I just felt I needed to be with my family. He sadly said he understood. I left and made the long-haul home.

When I arrived, I stuck my head in my parents' bedroom. It startled them awake. I whispered, "Hey, it's just me. I came home."

"Oh, okay," they replied. "Everything okay?"

"Yeah, just wanted to be home," I whispered.

I laid down in bed and like a kid anticipated the next morning of breakfast, gifts and family time on Christmas morning. I was glad I had decided to return home to familiarity. Suddenly, I was awakened by a gagging sound coming from the hallway. I jumped up to see where the noise was coming from. To my surprise, my dad was in the hallway, getting sick. I said, "Are you okay?" He was really sick and just continued to vomit, so I ran to grab him water. I knew he had some drinks at the Christmas gathering at my aunt's, so I figured he had too much and maybe had alcohol-poison.

When I returned with the water, he was crawling toward me on his hands and knees down the hallway and had made it to the living area a few feet from our lit-up Christmas tree. I bent down to try and give him water and he whispered, "I think I'm dying, Macy!"

"No!" I said back in a demanding way. I set the water beside him and told him, "I will call for help." I ran to the back of the house where my mom was sleeping soundly and woke my mom. As we round the corner of the hallway, we can hear a muffled grumbling sound coming from the hall bathroom again.

My dad was sitting on the toilet, door open and his color had gone from ghostly white to beet red. He was slobbering and incoherent as he continued to make grumbling sounds. I became frantic, as well as my mom, but I ran and called 911 as my mom continued to shout my dad's name. When I came back with the phone, my mom had started trying to pull him off the toilet onto the hall floor, but his weight was too much for her, so I helped her lay him flat slowly. I handed the phone off to her as the 911 operator was asking me to check his vitals. I needed to check his pulse and start CPR if he wasn't breathing, she said. I knew my mom wasn't trained in CPR like I had been in school, so I jumped into action. I was telling myself about the steps in my head like I remembered in health class, but it had been many years since I had taken the class and my memory was fading quickly amongst the chaos in my brain. I was checking his pulse, tilting his chin back to make sure he had a clear airway and starting the compressions. His faint pulse was fading away and his breathing had stopped as his face began turning blueish-gray. As I began transitioning from compressions to breaths, he let out a big sigh of tired, muffled breath that smelled like Jack Daniels liquor. To this day, I'll never smell dark liquor and not feel that night come racing back to me. I kept trying compressions, I was so tired, but I kept trying to start his heart. I did exactly like the 911 operator was telling me over the phone, and my mom was shouting and jumped down to try and give me a break finally. I was a mess inside, but I couldn't let it show. This could NOT be real life. No way!! I was frantically pacing and counting for my mom out loud while hyperventilating, crying and inside panicking. I jumped back in as my mom was getting winded. *OMG, he's losing this battle,* I thought, but I couldn't say it aloud. *Stop thinking that,* I told myself. *I must save him!* That's when my little sister, fourteen-year-old, Cameron, ran upstairs from her basement bedroom and stood in shock at the top of the stairs. No words, just tears falling and pure shock on her face.

The ambulance arrived and I was pushed toward my room with a sudden gush of men in the hallway of our home. I was alone and shouted, "Please help him!" I felt like I was shouting at myself like I was a ghost, and they couldn't even hear me. They ignored me while they went into action, giving meds directly to my dad's heart and trying to revive him. They joked at one point amongst one another like his life was meaningless and he was just another random man. I was furious! "HELP HIM!" I shouted again. I was helpless and just wanted this to end. *Why was this happening on Christmas morning to him? Why to my family?* As the paramedics and firefighters loaded him onto a stretcher, we all just collapsed from exhaustion, but we didn't have time to process all that was happening in front of us. They told us to follow them to the hospital. My mom grabbed her keys and told us to get in the car. As we followed behind the ambulance, we all sobbed uncontrollably. In my head, I was already apologizing to him. *I'm so sorry, I tried so hard, I'm so sorry, Daddy.* I knew it was the end in my head, but my heart was having a harder time processing the information. My mom was breathing heavily and said, "Girls, I just don't know. I think this is really bad." I could tell she was trying to be strong for us while also trying not to run off the road in a panic. As we arrived, they escorted us to a private waiting room near the emergency area. Thirty minutes or so went by and a doctor came in shaking his head with a sheer defeated look on his face. I dropped to my knees and let out more grief than I ever knew was possible. *Not my daddy. Not mine,* is all that kept repeating in my head. I looked at the doctor and said, "You go save him right now, RIGHT NOW!" As if ordering him would change the outcome. I didn't speak to my elders this way. I was raised to respect elders, but this was too much. I was beside myself with disbelief and sadness. My heart completely broke in half at that moment and any sort of manners went out the door too. I looked over at my firecracker of a Grandmother who stood just under 5ft tall in her 80s and in that moment, she became a frail, broken Mother who lost her will to live. She let out a cry that will haunt me till this day. Her youngest, seemingly healthy son was gone at the mere age of fifty-two from a massive heart attack on Christmas morning. She herself had survived many. The world was a cruel place. I ran outside to get air as the walls began to close in on me.

As I got outside, my little sister was standing there looking up at the sky in tears and silence. We embraced in a hug that I could close my eyes and still feel to this day. Tiny snowflakes fell on our faces as we stood there entangled in each other's grief, feeling so small in a world so big without our dad. At the moment, I felt like a five-year-old child left on a sidewalk alone to figure out the world. I remembered how I had yelled at the doctor, and something tugged at my heart. Maybe God, maybe my dad's spirit, was telling me to make amends. I went back into the hospital to find the doctor that gave me the worst news of my life thus far. After finding him, I tearfully apologized for shouting at him. I told him thank you for doing everything he possibly could. He became emotional as he held my hand and told me he tried everything and was so sorry. I know now that must be the worst part of being a doctor was losing a patient and having to tell the family. I don't know how looking back, I was able to find the courage to apologize to him, but I think at that moment, I took all the blame for my dad's death. It was my fault.

Chapter 3: Buried In Grief

I spent the next couple of days following in an out-of-body trance. I don't remember who was at our house, but I remember a lot of people coming and going. It's as if a revolving door was attached to the front of our home. I remember my best friend Lacy doing my makeup and hair for the funeral because I couldn't raise my arms to do it myself. I remember my older sister calling me from Old Navy to ask what size dress I wore because she was buying me something black to wear. I remember not being able to eat and having someone stick bites of food in my mouth. I shut down. I lost my will to carry on because the sadness consumed me. I didn't want to be here if my dad, who was my true best friend, wasn't. I didn't want to die at twenty years of age, but I couldn't imagine my life without him in it and this grief was too heavy. My tears ran dry from crying so much. Then suddenly, someone would say something that struck a chord inside my heart and a faucet of tears appeared & came out of my eyes from the depths of my soul.

The funeral was overwhelming, as though I was just watching myself like God granted me special permission to watch from my dad's perspective. As if I was seeing everything from his eyes. I watched how people reacted. I could hear whispers that they thought I couldn't hear, talking about my mom, my sister and I and the future we had in front of us without my dad. As people came and said many forms of condolences, "I'm so sorry if you need anything, let me know. He loved you so much, he was a good man. He will be missed. I sure loved your daddy." I faked a smile through the tears and just kept staring across the room at his casket. I wanted to go shake him and say, *WAKE UP!* Nothing was bringing him back and I knew that. Cameron had a hard time understanding death and the afterlife. She, at one point, wanted to go climb in the casket with our dad. My high school boyfriend, Mark, tried to console me. Cameron's boyfriend, Davin, tried to console her. Both were even Paul bearers who carried my dad to his final resting place. They both would hold a special place in our hearts for doing that forever. No one is prepared to lose a parent this young. Unfortunately, no matter what my boyfriend said or did, it wasn't enough. I had let down the one man who asked for my help when he was dying. I couldn't pretend like my life would ever be the same and I couldn't be happy with anyone, most of all myself. I wasn't capable of love at that moment or for many years after. I was lost. I was a shell of who I was.

As I stood there in that room of people before the funeral service began, I remember looking up and seeing a face that

I wasn't expecting to see, or maybe I just never considered how I would feel if he showed up. We stayed in touch on occasion, but he wasn't a part of my everyday life. The moment he walked in, everyone else disappeared into that room. He grinned, and then his grin turned to a somber set of eyes glaring back at me. Once our eyes locked, my footing became weak. My heart skipped and all of a sudden, my blood was pumping through my body again. I immediately wanted to run & fall into his arms. I wanted to disappear from all this and just lay in his arms in a quiet place and have him console me with the words only he could gather. My childhood guy best friend Paul stood there across the room, ready with open arms to help guide me through this pain. I walked over and just hugged him, but I was sure everyone could feel the energy shift. I just wanted my dad to reappear and everyone else to disappear except Paul. I suddenly remembered everyone's eyes were indeed on me. I thanked Paul for coming and backed away slowly. However, at that moment, that was all I needed. A strong energy-shifting hug that put life back into my body. No meaningless words, just someone to take the weight off my feet that understood the impact of us all losing my dad.

Shortly after, my dad's funeral began. My little sister began struggling with emotions on stage in the funeral chapel, so I got up and helped her finish what she had written for our dad. I remember jumping up without hesitation and trying to be her savior. I have no idea to this day what I said myself in front of such a large crowd. I hated public speaking, but for her and for our dad, I was willing to try. I remember looking out and seeing the saddest people I had ever seen, all hanging onto the words I spoke. God was nowhere when we all needed him, and the world was evil. The one solace of that day was that my dad had the biggest funeral procession I'd ever seen. Miles long stretching so far, we couldn't possibly see the end. He was a loved man, and so many should strive to leave that kind of legacy behind. He wasn't a man known for much, but he made a BIG, lasting impact on the ones he called family and friends and even acquaintances like his customers. In my mind, I had let a loved man die that Christmas morning and no one would ever truly forgive me.

Chapter 4: The Devil

When you are at your weakest, the Devil knows that's when it's time to attack. I was vulnerable and broken and most of the people around me were as well. I had just turned twenty-one that Spring. I was of legal age to drink now. I had spent years wishing this day would come as my boyfriend was three years older. Unfortunately, now I only wanted to get a bottle of vodka and go sit alone at my dad's gravesite, drowning my pain. I spent the next few years in a completely drunken stupor. Waking up with people mad at me for something I had done or said that I couldn't even remember. I had checked out from my relationship and was just trying my best to forget everything prior in my life. I partied. I danced. I clubbed. I didn't recognize myself anymore. I could only drink to feel nothing and that was good enough for me! I was tired of trying to pretend I was sober for the right people, like my bosses and family. I got kicked out of a bar for slapping my boyfriend that summer because he sat down with his buddies to chat with some girls.

I woke up the next day so sick from alcohol, not remembering but pieces from the night before. I had to be at work in an hour and I couldn't even get my head to raise up without the room still spinning. I would lose my job if I didn't go, I thought, so I sipped Gatorade. I threw my hair in a bun and dragged myself to the car. I sat in the room with two young kids, which I was held liable for as a nanny. I puked in one of their sand buckets. They toddled around me as they were so small. The smell of alcohol was still brewing in the air. I sprayed perfume but was so embarrassed and sat thinking, *what have I done to myself?* The room spun. My head pounded like a jackhammer was trying to break inside my skull. I ran and threw the bucket away in the warehouse trash can after I rinsed it. I knew I couldn't do my job and I knew something had to change in my life! I left work telling my boss that I felt like I had a virus. I went straight home and slept for the remainder of the day. I got up and called my mom later that night. I told her I was ready to move home. She decided to help me get my belongings that weekend. As we drove toward my apartment, the car radio began spinning uncontrollably. It wouldn't stop no matter what we pushed in the car. We had to pull over and turn the car off to get it to stop. I knew that my dad was communicating. I believe now he was letting us know his spirit was helping us. I couldn't even bare to tell my boyfriend as I couldn't explain how I felt after all these years together. He came home to a virtually empty apartment except for a bed and a sofa. I left a few necessities for him even though I had bought them. I apologized many years later, but to this day, I know I should have handled it better. *God, where were you when I needed you the most?*

Chapter 5: Lost & Found

I'd not taken a single second to be alone and grieve before I was drowning my sorrow in shots at clubs on the weekends still. I didn't know how to heal. My sister Cameron was preoccupied with her boyfriend and my mom was in a new relationship which I was anything but happy about. I spent the next several years jumping from one toxic relationship to another that ended with me feeling rejected and bitter. I remember thinking I was so far from who I used to be. When they say you must learn to love yourself before you can be in a healthy relationship, it's true. I moved out of state several times to try and forget all I had gone through. *Maybe a fresh start would help,* I thought each time. However, I was running from the pain and the pain kept following me because it was inside of me, not something following behind like a dark shadow I could shake off with distance. I assume that's how my sister and mom felt too. Lost with no direction. I knew deep down we were all miserable in our current lives. No matter what they did or where we went, the memories of my dad haunted them too. I spent the next several years trying to understand death by researching religion and spiritual side of life. Trying to figure out what all the signs I had gotten from my dad meant.

The fire alarm had gone off in the exact location he had his heart attack that next night after his passing. It sent us all into a scurry of panic, especially when it wouldn't go off at 2 am. The blinking lights inside our family home that kept happening, the tv coming on with a message from him days after he passed, the familiar songs on in the grocery stores on our birthdays, and the dreams I got often were all becoming clear that he wanted to pass on a message. His energy was around us, and he made it clear he wasn't just lying in the ground. His soul was very much still capable of making energy flow around us. This had to mean something. I buried my nose in books and internet findings. *Who was God? How could he let things like this happen? Could my dad's soul communicate through energy?* I was twenty-eight years old before I ever picked up a bible and tried to read it. I was desperately trying to find something worth living for and I felt the pull to understand him, our maker. After all, I heard he forgave you for your sins and I felt I needed forgiveness. I heard that he would love me even through this pain that was unbearable, and I needed strength. I heard that I'd be able to forgive myself and that his words could heal me. *Was it true?* It was worth diving into. So, I prayed and spoke to him, just him and I, alone and feeling I was heading in the right direction. But not in a go-to-church-every-

Sunday way where a preacher guided me. I worked on healing through true soul searching in my own quiet time way. I found myself in nature as I meditated on his word. My soul was tired and I needed to be revived. I needed to be restored, so I read the words in the bible. I researched what the words meant. I connected with so many messages. I suddenly felt a heaviness begin to lift from inside me slowly but surely. This burden I had carried for eight years was no longer just mine. He had his reasons for taking my dad early, and it wasn't up to me to understand or hold onto him any longer in anger. I learned to trust in my newfound faith. I found peace in knowing I wasn't alone and that I hadn't failed my dad. God simply needed him more but never left his side. The maker of all of us has predestined our lives. We all have an expiration date, and we must appreciate the love we can give while we are here. We must live in the moment joyfully, so we can have memories to hold onto of each other and ones we can leave behind. Like fingerprints on each person we come across. That is what life truly is about, the moments here on earth and, eventually, the forever place we will call home in the afterlife. Earth is just a part of our soul's journey, not the end. Now that I understand that, I'm at peace inside because I know that I will connect with all my loved ones again.

Shortly after, I learned to forgive myself for things that were totally out of my control, like my dad's death. God began what I like to call my series of blessings. I no longer found a need to drink or party. I found a man that helped me see my worth and I felt like he was the blessing I had been asking for. Someone to love me as I was with all my family baggage. Someone who could look past my flaws and work with me to help build who I was meant to become. He was patient and kind. He didn't ask much about my past and only wanted to look toward the future together. That Spring, he surprised me with a diamond engagement ring over brunch in bed. I said YES without hesitation! My heart was exploding with happiness. I relished in my excitement. I was finally getting my happiness.

Chapter 6: The Looming Gloom

My sister, Cameron, had just given birth a year earlier and was a new mom to a handsome baby boy. However, she'd not taken time to heal and or recover from our joint family trauma. She wouldn't be able to handle the responsibility like she thought. She quickly spiraled from dabbling in pain pills to the darker side of harder recreational drugs. When the pain pills didn't numb the pain of the grief, she found herself in a new world of scary drugs that would steal everything from her. A world that would give her highs from meth, cocaine, and eventually heroin, the true devilish dark side. I first noticed her struggling as she was attending cosmetology school and often said she was having a hard time balancing it all. Home, school and her new baby. So, my mom and I tried to help as much as possible. Cameron was now living with the father of her child but was home alone a lot and was completely reliant on him financially. She was trying to work her way through school, but the needs of her baby were interfering with her finishing. She decided to take a little time off but promised herself she would return. Then, she found out she was pregnant again. She decided, while she was pregnant this time to try and finish cosmetology school, and with some real dedication, was able to do just that. This time, she gave birth to a beautiful blonde-haired baby girl. I think the pressure of taking care of kids at the age of twenty-three, the dreams of her future slipping away and the heartache of missing her dad was all too much. Her high school friends, now away at college or starting their new careers, had left her empty. Most pretended to care, but she felt them pulling away and rarely got invited to anything. Her boyfriend was not someone she could count on. The water was often unpaid, the electricity was getting cut off for nonpayment and the food was becoming scarce in their home. So, she relied on my mom and me a lot. We would take turns bringing her what she needed. Diapers, formula, clothes for kids, car seats, medicine, and food were on a regular delivery service from one of us, the enablers. But, the responsibility of taking care of two children was becoming more than she could handle. As my mom dropped in for a surprise visit one day, when too long of time went without a reply on the phone, she found Cameron inside sleeping with the kids running freely in the home through toys and a mess of clothes. At first glance, she thought maybe she was just not feeling well, but when she found a needle wrapped in a shirt in their closet, she questioned her immediately. That's when the lies, the excuses and protecting her addiction came into play. She denied, denied, denied. Claiming at one point that her boyfriend was diabetic and that is where the needle came to be from. My mom was the wiser and called to tell me what she had found. I couldn't wrap my head around it. "Surely not. It must be from something else! Cameron would never do that to herself," I told her.

My mom took the kids home with her, and the search for finding help began. We found her, at best, a three-day maximum detox program that was state funded. However, she was an adult, so they immediately released her when she told them she wanted to leave and we weren't even notified. I spent hours on the phone calling to beg anyone who would listen to me to just give me directions. Most would say, "Call this number," which I had already done. A vicious circle of calling, redirecting, and a dead-end road to no real help. I felt totally lost and helpless. She deserved better! My dad would not give up on her, so I couldn't either. I had to leave the light of hope on. I had to let her know I was trying to help guide her, but that hope was quickly wearing thin. She needed a real rehab! Because Cameron had no insurance, that wasn't an option. Most legit drug recovery programs require upward of $15,000 and some require over $50,000, which the typical middle-class family doesn't have. None of us had experience with addiction and our pockets were quickly running dry from helping with the cost of the kid's needs. None of us knew that the word addiction would control our lives so much. I remember asking Cameron, *WHY? HOW? WHEN?* I don't believe she even had a clear answer about how it got to this point. But I had to understand how this beautiful sister of mine with a bright future was now a heroin addict, all while also being a Mom. The two do not mix, and I was having a hard time accepting her truth. I myself had lost five pregnancies to traumatic miscarriages in my twenties. I couldn't stand by and accept that the drugs came before anything. I was furious, bitter, sad, and wanted better for her. I wanted to have the person who had introduced her to these types of drugs put away for life! I wanted better for these innocent babies of hers. So, I did what any good aunt would do. I took them in. At the age of two and a half and thirteen months, the kids came to live with my new husband and me. I told her to go find help, and she knew she couldn't keep taking care of them in her current condition. So, she relentlessly turned them over to me and took off to another state with the father of the children and his best friend. She claimed she was getting better on the occasional phone calls we would receive.

The kids asked where Mommy was, and I would reassure them they would see her soon and Mommy was just at a place getting healthy. However, I rarely heard from her and her withdrawing so much I knew differently deep down. Then, I got a call five months later that she was coming back into town to get the kids. I cried thinking about their safety, but she promised she was clean and sober now and I didn't have legal custody, so I agreed. In the meantime, I went to see a custody lawyer. He said it was hard to prove a Mother was unfit and said all we had done was just merely give gifts to the children. I wasn't their Mom, and I wanted what was best for them, so I surrendered them back per the lawyer's advice. He claimed I could get a kidnapping charge against me if I tried to keep them without custody. Looking back, I should have required a drug test of her and her boyfriend. However, I was now pregnant with my first child, and after all my miscarriages, I was having some medical issues myself. I was struggling with the energy to keep up with two small kids and my own health and that of my unborn baby. As they drove off, I looked her in the eyes and said very seriously, "You better take good care of them. They deserve the best, Cameron." She agreed to call often, thanked me, and they were off faster than I could say goodbye. I was left with credit card debt from the care of the kids and a mountain of heartache, and all I got was a thank you. Part of me was relieved to be able to focus on my own pregnancy and my still very new marriage, and part of me felt immense guilt for letting them leave with their parents.

Chapter 7: Who Are You?

Some time had passed and we had seen my niece and nephew sparingly over those few months. My sister, her boyfriend and the kids were now living with my mom in the town I grew up. I was now about to be eight months pregnant and having my baby shower. So, I invited my sister to come. She came, and during the first hour of the party, she was upstairs in my bathroom, "getting ready", aka "getting high". When she arrived, I remember looking at her, thinking, *why are you so thin and fidgety?* But I quickly dismissed the thoughts she could be using. No way she could possibly be again with the kids around her all the time. Not in my mom's house would she be getting high. But my mom was now her full-time enabler and was secretly ashamed to be contributing to her growing addiction. Most parents are the enabler at some point in their child's addiction. After all, they just want their child to stay alive. So, they bend over backwards, doing anything they can to keep them on this earth. They give up their lives to tend to the addicts. Money for cigarettes, clothes, food, rides to wherever, and even raising their kids for them when they go MIA. I questioned my mom, and she would defend my sister at all costs. "No, she's doing good. She seems better now," she would say more times than I can count. I knew deep down otherwise, but I didn't want the rift in the family, so I ignored the obvious.

That March, my sister showed up to my daughter's first birthday so frail I thought she would break in half in front of my very eyes. With one look at her, I knew she was lying and completely lost in her addiction again. When she stayed in my bathroom upstairs for most of the party to finish, "getting ready". I knew that was code for "getting high". So, I went and told her to come down for the party because everyone was asking where she was and it was embarrassing. The door was locked and she wouldn't initially open it, so I banged on the door. She snapped and started a fight with me, saying I was being dramatic. I was furious and demanded she come down right now and told her I would not let her be involved in family gatherings at my home anymore if this was what I would deal with. She finally came down as I was in the backyard, speaking to friends. The look of guilt was written over her face and avoiding me at all costs. My mom carried on conversations to take the attention off my sister walking in late. *Cameron put on a good show,* she thought, smiling and jumping from one conversation to the next with our guests and family. Faking how happy she was and how good she was. She couldn't stay still; she often tapped her feet so badly from the nerve damage she had and the anxiety. She could care less. It was my daughter's only first birthday. She was oblivious that her getting high would be a constant memory I truly have of that day. She didn't even know my daughter on a personal level, so why was she there if all she was doing was getting high? When everyone left, I couldn't contain my anger and my emotions took over. I walked upstairs and took all her luggage and piled her belongings inside she had thrown all over my bathroom and bedroom. I got into a yelling match with her about how high she was and she burst into tears, saying I was the biggest bitch she knew. So, I opened my front door and threw out her suitcase and pushed her out my front door and shut it in her face and locked it. My mom immediately got upset with me, saying I was overreacting and that now Cameron would just run off and get high with someone else. Again, defending her choices and behavior. Not admitting Cameron had a problem was her way of protecting herself from admitting she had a drug-addict daughter. I was the problem, not my sister. The bitterness was setting into my core. I hated I was doing everything I could to maintain a normal life and I was the bad guy because I wasn't willing to deal with her addiction. Cameron called some stranger we didn't know to come to pick her up. The guy showed up happy as could be to even have a chance to spend with my sister getting high too. I was sick to my stomach that this was her life. I refused to give in. My boundaries as a Mom and aunt had to come first. Her drug use was her only focus. Her addiction was winning. I certainly felt like I was on the losing end. I was so angry at my sister. I was furious with my mom for continuing to go along with this behavior.

Chapter 8: Peace

I remember driving through the gates and feeling the calm that came over my entire body. I'd not seen anything so naturally beautiful still left essentially untouched by humans. The hardwood trees, green and lush, hung over the roads that flowed around the mountains and homes within this community. My husband and I were finally able to sneak away on the weekend alone without our daughter. I found this place on a suggested weekend getaway vacation internet search. I think now, after knowing what all this place would come to help in my future, I may have been led there by the divine. We spent the weekend exploring the many hiking trails. We ate at the restaurant overlooking a golf course strategically placed amongst the jaw-dropping mountain backdrop. The sun was setting just as we arrived, just as we sat on the balcony, and it was a beautiful evening of ambiance and good food. As we went back to the cabin we rented, I couldn't help but want to know more about this place. It was a hidden gem that many had never heard of, even me, a Georgia native. I suddenly came across homes that were very expensive and I admired their beauty and said, "Well, maybe one day." That's when by chance, I ran across a home that was on the older side but had unique architecture. *The price was too good to be true,* I thought. Much lower than anything else in this community. Perhaps it just needed a little work? I showed my husband and he agreed we would try to see it in person before we left that weekend. I called the realtor, and she was willing to show us on Sunday. As we pulled up to the home, I immediately got excited inside, but I knew this was still a long off-goal. So, I contained my excitement. We were just there window shopping. As we stepped down the cobblestone walk away, I felt like I was walking into a camping lodge. The trees all towered way above our heads and I could hear the birds' whistling overhead. *How serene!* We stepped inside, and I felt like it needed some work, but nothing too crazy. The hardwood floors and open living room with windows surrounding the nature just outside was a winning feature. *Nothing we couldn't conquer over time,* I thought. That's when I saw the excitement on my husband's smiley face. He was feeling the same way I was. Happy. The home was something that allowed us to grow as a family, which we slowly needed. However, the outside environment was what sold me. I could step outside and feel like I was in a state park, in quiet, in peace. As we left the appointment to view this home, I couldn't help but instantly pull out my husband's feelings on what he thought. He agreed it was really amazing. The pools, the trails and the amenities would be so wonderful for our daughter to experience. The lifestyle change would be a bit tricky. Although my husband worked from home, he still would be called into work on occasion and that would mean driving an hour and half into the city. That night as we arrived back home, we sat for dinner. I looked around me, and I couldn't help the feeling of wanting to run back to the peaceful place we had just enjoyed that weekend. I said aloud, "But why do we have to live like other people expect? Why can't we do something crazy and move to the mountains and live under the trees with the animals?"

My husband smirked and, being the logical one, said, "But how Macy? How on earth could we possibly make this work? We don't even know if they have internet service up there that would accommodate my job."

I frowned, and I suggested, "We can always call and check. Surely others work from home." He agreed, and the next morning he came to me saying he found out the internet provider would, in fact, work for him.

"Wait, are you saying what I think you are?"

My husband replied hesitantly, "Yes, let's check into some realtors and see what we could get for this house."

I couldn't believe it! This was all happening; we may be moving to the mountains! Before we could blink, our home was on the market, the offer was accepted and we were off to live in the mountains of North Georgia.

Chapter 9: The First Attempt

Moving to a new area meant leaving friends and even family behind, but my husband and I were both ready. I think part of me just needed a fresh start. I needed a new town, new faces, and less stress. After all, our original home was just a short drive to my mom's/sister's home and the looming darkness that was taking over my sister's life. I couldn't be in the heat of it anymore. I wanted to focus on being the best me, a good Mom, and work on my healing from the trauma my younger years had projected on me.

The stress of everything I'd been through was dying to escape my body. The holidays in this community were like magic here. Trunk or treats with costume contests that my daughter won for dressing as a unicorn. Oktoberfest with festival activities complete with food trucks, a Christmas lighting of the tree with Santa and his sleigh and our first snow that winter was nothing short of magic too. But July 4th was spectacular and still a favorite time. The fireworks were big and lasted for a while. During the day, everyone was at the pool overlooking the lake activities like kayaking, paddle boarding, and canoeing. They had a live bongo player that made it feel like a vacation was being had. We had deer who frequented our yard. Black bears with cubs made their way through our yard and stopped to smell what we were cooking. We had owls in the trees nearby who made noises at us often. We had a fox go trotting right past our driveway one time as we pulled up from a run to the store. A bobcat crossed in front of the car while driving down the mountain one time, and so much more exciting things. I swear I lived in a fairy tale. I met wonderful girlfriends. I finally had a village of other mom friends who were supportive and offered positive advice. I spent my Sundays doing yoga at a top mountain home of a dear friend of mine. It overlooked it all and when you stepped into that space, you could feel the healing taking place. Through meditation, I was able to find the things I needed to heal. I was able to find my needs, wants and desires, and forgiveness. It was all really good until it wasn't. Despite me having the ability to lock my sister out via our community security gate. My heart was having a harder time keeping her away. I missed my sister. I was missing valuable memories I'd never get back. The kids had a relationship with us because I put the effort in to keep it that way. With her, I had a giant wall up. I often invited my mom and the kids up or went to get them for the summer. However, no one was dealing with the fact that my sister was frail, thin again, and completely lying about everything happening in her life to us and, most of all, her kids and herself. She was in the pit of her addiction and dying slowly. My mom called to tell me Cameron was having seizures from the drug use and was often in emotional turmoil from dealing with her every day. I would get on the phone, yet again trying to find some help, only to run into brick walls everywhere I turned. I didn't know how to help. I didn't have the means to pay for rehab. The only thing I ever found was a short detox. No REAL help for her. I didn't want to even think of it. The haunting feeling was becoming clearer. I very well could be burying my little sister. She would lose her battle eventually if this continued. So many we knew from school had lost their battles with addiction. Then, we found out my grandmother was not doing well. My uncle requested my mom move to Charleston, South Carolina, to help take care of her as she had become bed bound after a fall that broke her hip. I knew I didn't want my family so far away, but I also thought this could be a fresh start for my mom or possibly even my sister and the kids. So, I encouraged her to go.

My uncle rented a house big enough for all of them and set my grandmother up to be comfortable at home. Her dementia was taking over her body, but her brain was aware of most things, including who we were. She enjoyed being in the home with my mom and sister and the kids would often go tease her and sit with her, which she enjoyed. I'd drive to Charleston every few months to visit, too and have my daughter in tow. Until I found out I was pregnant with my son. I focused on the health of my baby and my own needs as I was struggling with extreme nausea and problems that could risk my baby's future. I was then put on bed rest. So, I stayed away from the stress. I found out my sister had gotten a job and my mom assured me she was sober for the first time since our dad passed. *I couldn't believe it!* But I was just happy that things were heading in the right direction. *False hope.* I thought, *wow, she will beat this awful beast. Her first try at recovery and I knew she had it in her!*

Chapter 10: Too Good To Be True

When I got a call that my grandmother was in her last days, I, without hesitation, jumped in the car with my baby girl and headed to Charleston. When we arrived, she was already in a coma state of consciousness upstairs in her hospital bed. She wasn't responding to touch or sound and had her eyes remained closed and mouth faintly open. Her breathing became shallower by the hours that passed. My sister and I sang to her for hours a song about angels knowing how lucky they are to have her. We knew it wouldn't be long, and we tried our best to let her know she was loved and her next step would be meeting her maker.

The next morning my sister had to be at work, so she left even though she didn't want to go. My mom and I sat in the room next to my grandmother and spoke of memories. We laughed, we cried, and we hung on to every breath. I could see in my mom's face how nervous she was to have to say goodbye. There was a lot unsaid. Her family never spoke of emotions. They never hugged or showed much love. So, I encouraged her to talk to her alone. I didn't want things left unsaid and I believed, at that moment, my grandmother could still hear us. A state of being asleep and awake and in the next realm is where I believe she lingered. My uncles slowly poured in one at a time and began spending time with her. I would go in and hold her hand and stroke her face and tell her it was okay to go if she was hurting too much. I told her she had done so well fighting and loving all of us. I told her she was always going to be someone I cherished dearly and that I would always keep her with me and would miss her more than words. I thanked her for the time she spent with me as a child and for helping form me as a woman with my own opinions. My mom also told her it was okay to go. I hated seeing my spunky and silly grandmother lifeless. Alzheimer's is truly a disease like no other. It really does slowly steal the person from you. Just then, her amazing part-time nurse Ruth arrived to do her daily check. Her breathing changed to a death rattle. If you've never heard this, you are lucky. She ran from the bathroom to the room as soon as she heard. My mom and Ruth began to give her morphine and her mouth opened wider as if to let one last giant breath inside of her failing body. I grabbed her hand and I just kept telling her, *it's okay. It's okay to go. I love you so much, Grandmom.* Tears fell like a river around us all. Ruth ran to the window and opened it. She said her soul needed to be free to go where it was going next. I'd never heard of this, I loved how compassionate and thoughtful she was to my grandmother, but at that moment, I realized why she did this. I realized she was a soul releaser. Not just anyone had this ability, but Ruth did. She was special, and she was so needed in that room with us. I will forever be thankful for her love and kindness. She was a light in the darkness.

That night my husband finally arrived and we were lying in bed with our daughter, who was one and a half in between us. As we started to dose off to sleep, she reached her hands in the air straight up. Her eyes remained closed and she was in what looked like a dream. It woke my husband and me up and we just looked at one another and stared down at her. That's when she spoke clearly, saying, "Bye-bye, Grandmom," and waved her hands into the air. My grandmother's soul had come to say goodbye, and the goosebumps sent every single hair on my body standing for the remainder of the night.

Chapter 11: Too Much Grief

As the other family members began coming in and the coroner was notified, the grief overwhelmed me. My daughter was sitting in the room with my niece playing and I kept the door closed and music on to distract from all that was happening in the other part of the home. But, once I checked in with them and called my husband and told him to get there asap. I sat in a chair and I let out my grief and cried so hard. I was so tired of losing the people I loved. I was tired of saying goodbye. My heart hurt so much. I contorted my body like a pretzel, buried my head in my hands and just let all the feelings flow that I had held onto stay strong in front of my family. My aunt Jenna, who was close to my grandmother, came running up when she received the news. She came and put her hand on my shoulder and we both wept as we grieved for my grandmother's loss. Life would be forever different without her in our lives, and we all knew it. She was the glue, as often the matriarchs are.

As we called Cameron, she raced home but also was so sad to know she wasn't there in her last moments. I think it was all too much to handle another grief so great. As months passed, my sister decided to let her kids' biological Dad to come live with them. I thought it was a horrible idea because

I felt my mom would just be taken advantage of again. However, my mom decided to move back to Georgia and try to rekindle her relationship with her longtime boyfriend, Keith. So, she left my sister, her boyfriend and their kids to finish out the lease at the house they lived in.

Several months later, my mom told us that Keith found out he had melanoma cancer. I was now seven months pregnant and my sister was still in Charleston, SC. My mom said that she had to get down and make sure they moved out of the rental home in time for the lease to end. She had suspicions that they were using again together and was scared to see the state of the house. She arrived and it was absolutely a disarray. They weren't packed at all. The house needed cleaning up and they were in no shape to move out. My sister was now the thinnest she had ever been. Her cheekbones were showing and her hip bones were now poked out of her sides. Her hair was thinning and she had sores on her face. My mom was in disbelief as she called to tell me the news. She needed help and Keith was in no condition to help them move. So, I packed up without my husband's approval, seven months pregnant and made the drive to help my mom. I knew I couldn't help more than take the kids away. I couldn't lift and put my life or that of my babies in danger. So, I rented a hotel room nearby, and I took the kids there to give them baths. My niece had a horrible ear infection and was so sick that she was in tears. I was so mad that I couldn't see straight. I hated my sister. I hated the Dad who came into their lives to wreck them even more. That's when I learned from the kids that their Dad had overdosed in front of them recently. They said they had to run to the neighbors' house for help calling 911 as my sister tried to revive him. So, not only were they using, but they were now dying in front of them. *How could my sister be this bad off?* To not care that her children had to witness death, drug use, and who knows what else. *What kind of person does this? An addict.* An addict's brain is so warped they don't see passed that next fix. She refused to let anyone take them, and I kept telling her soon the state would be involved if she didn't straighten her life out. I was now beginning to have stomach pains, and was regretting going at all. I was in no condition to be dealing with this stress. I called my husband, who was growing angry by the second for me going to try and help in my current condition. I cried and told him I just wanted to bring the kids back home again. He forbid it and said, "I don't know what to tell you to do, but you're about to have our son. You cannot bring them back. Can't your Mom take them?"

I told my sister I was going to just bring them back. She fought with me and threw the kids in the car with her and her boyfriend and drove off. I called and reported her vehicle. But I didn't know the tag number, so they never located them. I was forced to come back home, completely unhinged emotionally and worried sick over my niece and nephew. I knew my sister thought I was going to take them forever, and I would have… but I didn't have the fight left.

A few weeks later, they ran out of money or resources and came back to Georgia. I was so relieved to have them closer and safe. They were temporarily staying with their other Grandmother. We didn't have open communication, but I trusted they were being cared for better than they had been. My sister was floating from that house to my mom's and whatever place she could land for the night. The Dad of her two kids, still in active addiction himself, couldn't help. Two women fighting for their adult children to just take care of their grandkids and get sober. Two bitter moms blamed one another's adult children for the other's addiction. Both enablers and both refused to see they had to do something to end this or cut ties and do what was best for their grandkids. I was now seven and a half weeks pregnant when I got a call that my sister was arrested for drug charges. She began paying for her choices and it would haunt her for a long time to come. She called, begging me to get her out of jail. She begged my mom over and over to bail her out of the jail and laid the guilt trip on thick. She knew pulling at her heartstrings would weigh eventually. I told my mom not to dare get her out. I said if she gets out, she will just go get high. She needs time to detox and to realize her actions have a cost. My mom, I could tell, was struggling not to run to her rescue. But I kept reminding her this is what is best for Cameron. A week later, she was still in jail. She finally saw we were all just sick of living this life with her. We didn't sign up for it, and we could just walk away.

Chapter 12: The Son & the Holy Spirit

I woke up and was planning to have lunch with my mom on her birthday. As I stepped into the shower, my water broke. At first, I thought, how did I pee myself? Suddenly I realized I was in labor. I took a quick shower to rinse off and got dressed. As I went downstairs slowly, I told my husband to call the doctor. The next few hours were extremely stressful. I kept telling myself to breathe, but I knew I had to have an emergency C-section for a second time as I had previously gone through a uterine myomectomy to remove fibroids and natural labor wasn't an option for me.

As we drove to the hospital with my daughter in tow, the contractions were growing more intense and getting closer together. Now five minutes apart. My mom and in-laws and sister-in-law would meet us at the hospital. I was scared we wouldn't make it. I was rushed back and immediately they checked and I was 5cm. They scrambled all around me, checking blood, getting history, etc. My epidural had me feeling woozy and faint, so they waved alcohol wipes in front of my nose to keep me awake. It worked and I kept as still as humanly possible while they inserted the needle in as I sat on the edge of the bed bent over. It was a clammy feeling, but I managed to hang on. Next, I was in the room with bright lights in my face and being scooted onto the operating table with the draped sheet over me. They started the C-section and I knew something was not right. I yelled that I could fill it. They hushed me, saying I would feel some pinching and maybe pulling but nothing more. I assured them it was more than that! I could feel every single bit of the pain, the touching, the cutting, omg I can feel more. As they delivered my son, I screamed in pain and told them I didn't feel good and I felt all that was happening. Just as my sons' face was shown to me, I let out another excruciating scream. That's when they knocked me out cold with full anesthesia. I woke up alone in recovery feeling so confused, and I remembered saying something to the doctor in my dream right after they knocked me out to the effect, "Oh, you will put me together like Humpty dumpty?" I'm obviously hallucinating from lack of blood. I cried out, "Hello?" The nurse appeared and told me my husband was down in the NICU while they were checking out our son. He was just being checked since he was six weeks early, she assured me. But something in my mama heart felt wrong. I was thankful when my husband finally came back to update me. He said that he was a big healthy boy at 7lbs 11 oz. He said that they were concerned with his breathing a little and thinking he just needed time to clear the fluid. I knew this was common, so I didn't panic yet. But, after I was placed in a normal hospital room on the labor and delivery floor and six hours had passed and no one was giving me more information, I got very upset. I hadn't held my baby or nursed like I wanted, and when I called the NICU they just said that he was stable. What does this mean? Why hadn't anyone come up to tell me more about what he was dealing with? Was everyone just lying? That's when the warm liquid felt soaked through the back of my hospital gown. My pain level was so intense I knew something was awry. We called the nurse, she came and checked my epidural. "OH!" she gasped.

"Omg, what now," I replied.

"Your epidural is completely out of you. I will have to remove it and just get you pain medicine orally." I just had a C-section without an epidural. I knew that what I had felt was anything but normal, but I never imagined I was being cut open while my epidural was slowly wearing off! I looked at my husband, who, by his facial expression, understood why I was screaming during delivery even clearer.

I said, "Just take it out and let me go see my baby. I can handle pain now."

She told me I had to remain in bed for a certain time and then they would wheel me down to the NICU. More hours passed and I kept pushing to be taken to the NICU. Finally, at nearly midnight, they showed up with a wheelchair. I got to my baby boy finally and he was perfect. He had dark black hair combed into a mohawk. He had big blue eyes that peered at me and I told him I was so sorry it took Mommy so long to get there. I said you are so strong, my sweet boy. His tiny fingers gripped my hand and I was completely in love.

The doctor came from behind the curtain and wanted to update us. He explained that his spleen was enlarged and that he was having a tough time eating, so they had feeding tubes there to help with that to ensure he got the right nutrients. I told him I wanted to nurse and he encouraged me to pump and bring the liquid gold to them to run through the machines. He said more lab tests needed to be performed before they could diagnose. I was now sick with worry. He told us he would be back the next morning around 8 am to go over the results. They told us that he was fighting jaundice and that our blood types were incompatible with Rh incompatibility. Basically, my blood was fighting his the entire time and treating his tiny body like a foreign object. Even though obviously, not in my control, I felt immense guilt. My poor baby! He would spend the next three weeks in the NICU. My husband and I were staying at Ronald McDonald's house, going back and forth to visit and drop breastmilk. I didn't have one second to heal from my traumatic C-section. I was thrown into having a child who needed me at the hospital while also worrying about my three and half year old child, who was bouncing back and forth between my mom and my in-laws. I was sure she thought we abandoned her for the new baby. Although I knew our moms loved on her, it wasn't me. I was pumping around the clock to keep my supply up, which in the midst of stress, was anything but easy. I put my superhero cape on, though, my head down and focused on trying to help my boy get better. I did what was needed, which was to provide him with the healthiest milk I could produce. Finally, a new doctor was put on my son's team and she called me just as I had left visiting him and was about to lay down to rest. She explained that in her experience, babies who were slow to eat on their own and still struggling with anemia, jaundice and just generally looked like they didn't feel good, it was a good idea to move forward with a blood transfusion. I was hesitant, but I listened to her advice and told her to go ahead. We rushed back over to the hospital and stayed while they prepped him for the transfusion. I was emotional and just concerned with all his tiny body was having to go through. I was thankful he would grow to not remember this one day. I kept focused on getting him home healthy. By the next morning, he was like a different baby. I nursed him and he took to it immediately hungry. I was so relieved. A step in the right direction! I was so thankful for this new doctor! I left that afternoon to finally go rest and planned to come back later that evening to nurse again. I was still pumping around the clock, but I was exhausted and all the emotions I was holding inside needed to come out. I got back to the room and took a shower, and I could hardly contain myself. I let the water run over my healing painful incisions from C-section surgery. The water stung my painful breast that throbbed from pumping so much. I cried out, thanking God for helping my boy through this time. I thanked him for giving me the strength to make it through this. I knew I would be taking him home soon and at that moment, the weight on my shoulders became lighter. I handed him the torch to guide me through this life. Looking back, I think I was so desperate for something to just lift some of that pressure to fix such a hard situation off my shoulders. I would have done anything. Another moment when I was so desperate to feel supported by something bigger than myself I dropped to my knees. I decided then I would be thankful not just in my times of need but for all my blessings, both big and small. It was obvious I had blessings all around me,

and they weren't just coming from nowhere. God never left
me in my time of need.

Chapter 13: Understanding the Impact

I think going through with loss of loved ones, literally holding them as they took their last breaths, has lasting effects on you. I immediately took on the responsibility of feeling I could have done more to help them survive. But it wasn't my fault and I eventually learned to let that blame on myself go. Going through my sister's addiction made me thankful that I pulled myself from the grief sooner and didn't succumb to the life of addiction myself with my drinking. It could easily have been me instead. In the years after my family member's passing, I definitely had to find healthy ways to deal with that loss. They were a big part of my life and learning to live without them was anything but easy. One healthy way I found to deal with that grief was through doing volunteer projects. Cooking for people was a love language to me and it helped me keep their memory alive. After all, food was a big part of our family events. I also chose to do things in their memory. Like raising money for American Heart Association at my wedding and on social media for birthday fundraisers. I watched family movies with my kids to keep their memory alive every so often. I read self-help books that helped me understand the power of positivity. What I went through with five miscarriages, two emergency

C-sections, four fertility surgeries including ruptured ovarian cyst laparoscopy at twenty-three, fibroid removal via myomectomy at twenty-eight, a failed uterine ablation at thirty-eight, and finally, a hysterectomy at forty would have been far worse had I not kept a positive attitude surrounding those circumstances. I would never have been able to overcome this if I hadn't been forced to find my own inner strength early on and find sobriety for myself, either. Healing my physical health was an important part of healing my mental health and healing my mental health allowed me to heal my emotional trauma.

My medical pitfalls forced me to want to learn more about how my own body works, more than just the physical effects stress and trauma can cause. It forced me to look at other people with more compassion because I know mental health is so important and can quickly consume you if it's off balance. My body has gone through a lot, and it came out stronger but the route to get to the healing was anything but easy. Nothing worth overcoming is ever easy. It's given me a newfound sense of appreciation for all my body has been able to handle emotionally, physically, and mentally. I found myself diving into a world of supplements and different practices of meditation focused on surrounding myself with positive people and events and finally, writing to share my story has also been therapeutic. I started saying yes to things I wanted more and no to things that didn't get me to my goals. I surrounded myself with like-minded positive people and removed negativity. I realized I had to stop carrying the choices of my sister, Cameron, and focus on my own journey. It forced me into a deep self-reflection and made me forgive myself for where I felt I fell short in life. I had to sort through emotions that I hadn't dealt with and one of those was the bitterness and hated that my sister's addiction had brought into my heart. Her choices impacted me negatively for many years. The stress likely took years of my own life away. It was easy to tell myself I wouldn't let her stress affect me. It was another practice to find ways to not allow it to affect me. Was I ready to flip the light off on my sister? Was it truly hopeless like I felt? No, I couldn't give up hope her life would change too. So, that light stayed on, but I did it with boundaries this time. I wouldn't allow her at family gatherings. I could safely keep her at arm's length and not allow her into my space of my home. I stuck to that boundary. I tried sending encouraging messages, thinking somehow it would help her know I still loved her but couldn't involve myself with her continued addiction. It worked, for a while to help me maintain a certain level of calm. I just was pretending to be left in the dark. I told my mom that my boundaries were there to protect my family and me. I wouldn't allow my sister's stress to consume me like years earlier. So, I asked her, please don't call to tell me about my sister's problems. I said if you chose to stay in it and keep enabling, then you are on your own. I pulled my blindfolds on and kept busy. Unfortunately, my mom would call, saying she had had enough of my sister's shenanigans and couldn't keep doing it alone. She would say that family doesn't give up on family and that I was horrible for even considering giving up. The guilt would set in and I would be drawn back into the drama. My sister was slipping back into addiction again. I received a call that she had OD'd and my mom was hysterical, saying she had given her CPR to keep her alive and the kids witnessed it. I was furious. I immediately got in the car and went to get the kids. They stayed with me for a week while my sister went into detox. She got out and did good for a while. It was the longest she had ever maintained a sober life since the age of fourteen. We were going on nine months sober with her! So, I decided to plan a girl's day for me and her to celebrate. I wanted to let her know that I was so very proud of her dedication to sobriety! She was counseling, taking prescribed medicines, and working on herself. So, I took her to get a massage and out to lunch. We spent the day laughing and making up for a lost time as sisters. I was so happy to see this new Cameron. I went home that day and just cried, letting years upon years of stress leave my body. This is the relationship I wanted for her and me. This is what I missed! Surely this wasn't too good to be true? But knowing the statistics, I couldn't help but question her authenticity even in the best times.

Chapter 14: Too Much This Time

That winter, I decided to host a painting event at my home with some family and girlfriends. I decided it was time to let my sister join in the fun, so I also invited her. She showed up, but I could tell she was feeling under the weather. She claimed she was still recovering from the flu the week prior. So, I gave her some ibuprofen and we all started our painting projects. During this, she claimed she needed to go outside and get fresh air as she was beginning to not feel well. We all finished our projects. Cameron was still MIA. My eldest half-sister Makayla had just arrived as we were planning to do a wine tasting and dinner next. My sister Cameron said she would be happy to be the designated driver as she wasn't drinking and was sticking to her sobriety.

When some time had passed, my mom approached me, saying that she couldn't find Cameron anywhere. I laughed and said, "She was likely walking around smoking or asleep in the basement."

She said, "No, I've looked, and she's nowhere."

I was showing Makayla around my new house, as she'd never visited. I reached the door to the basement a few minutes later. I was talking and stopped as I heard what sounded like screaming. It was hard to make out where exactly it was coming from. I opened the door leading to my basement and heard the most God-awful cry for help. I knew immediately it was Cameron. I looked back at my sister Makayla and my friend Kacy and screamed for my husband to keep our children in our bedroom door closed no matter what. I nearly fell down the stairs trying to run down to get to my mom and Cameron. When I turned the corner, I could hear my mom's cry coming from the bathroom. I turned the corner and Cameron was lying on her back and was puffy and foaming at the mouth. I immediately told my mom to back up and I started putting cold water from the nearby sink on Cameron's cheeks. She was completely drenched in sweat yet clammy to the touch and feverish. I started screaming, "Wakeup Cameron, don't do this to us! Don't do this to your kids, damnit, wake up right now! OMG WAKE UP!" I couldn't believe what I was seeing. My sister was dying in my arms, just like my dad… only from an overdose. I was immediately so overtaken with sadness that I couldn't contain my emotions. I was sobbing while hyperventilating. My friend Kacy was in the medical field and was certified in CPR. So, my eldest sister Makayla called 911 while we began CPR together. Taking turns from sheer exhaustion but going as hard as we could each time. One was doing compressions while the other was counting. I couldn't let my sister die. I couldn't allow this to happen on my clock again, and not in my home! Finally, the paramedics arrived, and they administered Narcan. Something I never imagined I would need to consider having in my home, an antidote to heroin. A wake up and live drug, if given in enough time, could save an opioid overdose. I immediately looked at my mom and said I need air; I was slowly suffocating. The room was closing in, I was nauseated and I had a full-blown panic attack.

Makayla joined us outside in tears and just kept saying, "Why would she do this?"

I replied, saying, "I just can't believe this. I just celebrated her sobriety two weeks ago! TWO WEEKS! WHY?" I didn't know if my sister was even alive. I couldn't take a breath. That's when Kacy, also very emotional, came out and said the Narcan had woken her back up and she was irritated but responsive. I was so angry, so damn angry at my sister. I had done all the right things, I felt this time. I even told her if you ever feel the need to go use it, call me! Call me so I can talk you off the ledge! I'll be that person you can be honest with, but don't leave me questioning if you're sober again. Again, she was taken to the emergency room, and the doctor suggested none other than a detox. Why is there not more help, I always wondered. It's so broken. I couldn't live this way anymore. I was so exhausted and had promised myself I wouldn't let her drug use affect me anymore. I allowed her into my home, and this is what she did… in my children's presence. Although they didn't witness it, they heard the screaming. I was so mad I couldn't see straight. The hate that consumed me was too much. I spent the next several days in a daze and puddle of tears. I blamed myself. Maybe I expected too much of her too fast. Maybe she wasn't ready to be involved in family events. That darn anger, though, was too much. I felt it eating away at my heart.

When my daughter, then five, came to me saying she was scared to go to school and leave me because I was so sad… I knew I had to do something for myself. I couldn't keep on this road with Cameron. So, I decided to find a support group for family members of addicts. That's when I found Naranon and told my husband I was going to attend the next meeting, which was that evening at a local church. That night I learned what boundaries were. I even invited my best friend to join me the next week. I learned that I needed to focus on myself and I had no control over my addict family member. I learned that I wasn't alone and this is far too often the case. We get to a point where no matter how much we love the addict, we just can't keep allowing their negative choices to affect our mental health and our well-being. I was at my lowest. I kept reliving that moment of me begging her to wake up. I was so angry at my mom too. She was completely consumed by Cameron's lifestyle. She bent over backward to make sure Cameron stayed alive, but it was clear it was killing us all. I left that first meeting, realizing that I would never again be able to fully trust Cameron. No matter the time that went by, my guard would have to be up forever. I knew she could always pull the rug out from all of us. So, I kept going to those meetings. I kept learning more about addiction. I invited my mom, but she refused. Seeing her contribution to my sister's addiction was too close for comfort. She had never been someone who could admit wrong, and this wouldn't be any different. I didn't blame anyone but my sister. However, I did feel our mom had spent so many years denying that she was helping her stay an addict. She always kept a roof over her head and I knew Cameron needed to know she had no one or nothing to really want to change. When she lost it all, she surely would change then. I had lost hope after that last incident. I didn't believe anything she said. I questioned if she ever was sober, but I decided she was in fact the day we did sisters sobriety day. She was, I wasn't wrong in celebrating but now she had nearly succumbed to her addiction right in my home. I'd never trust her again and she knew it.

The truth was too much, and I think she knew the disappointment she had in herself, her children, and the rest of us was going to be her excuse the next time. Before we knew it, she was disappearing with the father of her children to go get high and lying like clockwork. We were all too familiar with this road. That's when I got a call that she had been in a horrible car crash with the father of her children, who was driving. The car flipped and they were in a completely totaled car that sent them both into emergency surgeries. We weren't sure that either of them would even survive. Finally, we received news they were stable. Both were lucky to be alive, and still, denying drugs was the reason. Cameron had to endure a major back surgery and was enduring immense pain. I thought either this was a wake up call or this was a new way for her to get pain pills and she would die from that now. I picked her up from the hospital and told myself to stay calm, but the emotions overcame me and I gave her a very stern lecture on the drive to drop her at home. I told her I was so disappointed in her choices. We all knew she and the father of her kids being around one another was like fire and gas, an explosion waiting to happen. I told her there was no way she could keep doing this to herself, or it was going to end in death. I very boldly told her we wouldn't be continuing to have a relationship if this was how poorly she cared for all of us and our well-being! Surely almost dying in a car accident and sending your kids into a panic of worry, our mom nearly having a heart attack from constant worry and affecting your sister this much was enough to break this horrible cycle! She cried and just told me she knew she was lucky. She'd spend the next few weeks recovering at my mom's home from the accident and her recent back surgery. The emotional side came out. The most famous sentence an addict will ever say, and you wished they meant, came out of her mouth, "I'll never ever do it again!" She pleaded with everyone about how much she meant it this time. Always apologetic during the detox and right after. They were always sorry when the truth slapped them in the face that they had let everyone down, most of all themselves. I'm sure that was a hard thing to face, that you had, in fact, let yourself down and thrown away your sobriety. Knowing how it would end but not being able to say no. I know it had to be very hard to look at yourself in the mirror. I can't even imagine looking at the disappointed faces of my children, my mom, and my sisters, who would literally do anything for you. It's a vicious cycle. You overcome the addiction for a while; everything is going well, the white cloud phase they call it. Then, real life happens, something hard emotionally drops in to say hello… a job loss, a car wreck, or some other misfortune and suddenly, you can't deal with life. You have zero ability to cope with stress. You're go-to is to turn to drugs to numb, but you can't if you want to maintain sobriety. That feeling pulling at you because of the changes that have happened in your brain are overwhelming. So, you say, I'll just do it once, just to make this not feel so stressful, but then guess what? You feel so good and it's made you forget you have anything bad happening. So, you say, *okay, fine, just one MORE time.* The cycle of addiction. That's why it's so important, so very important for the addict to find ways to deal with stress. To learn their boundaries and learn their limits. If a situation stresses you out, if a person stresses you out, then you can no longer involve yourself in those situations with those people. It's absolutely vital to say no to anything that could lead you back to that former life. Healthy forms of self-care through exercise, healthy ways to communicate with people they trust, being able to express themselves through creativity, managing balanced medication if needed, and staying involved in some kind of recovery program, whether it be inpatient or outpatient or online support groups. Without it, they lack the direction to stay on the right path to sobriety. Balance, consistency, and steady goals are a must for a recovering addict. Really for all of us, it's a must for the rest of our lives. As soon as they start to steer away from the things that helped them get sober in the first place, that's when the devil strikes again. I watched my sister struggle with this over and over. The vicious cycle kept pulling her back.

Chapter 15: You Weren't Born With Nine Lives

We all are given one life. One life to make it what we want. Our circumstances form our way of thinking, and at times it's hard to separate what we've learned through facing trials and what we need. As an addict, my sister watched death early on, but so did I. What made her and I different was; I was able to pull myself away from alcohol and focus on the positive thing in life. I focused on keeping my dad's memory alive with the ways he contributed when he was alive. My sister focused on losing him and why God would ever let her down if he really loved her. Sometimes I think she pushed her limits of addiction to see if God would keep blessing her by waking her back up. Maybe she needed that validation from him that her days weren't meant to end yet. Maybe she needed to know her actions weren't going to be what her life would end with and that acting out and harming herself wasn't going to end well. She wasn't born with nine lives; she was only given one. The sooner she was able to see this, the quicker she would be able to find recovery. I knew deep down that rock bottom, for her, was death. She had come close several times. What was it going to take to get her to wake up from this life she led and find a new way to live? I think the first step is to take away the one thing I knew she loved the most… her children, but this time, move them away so far it would take work for her to see them. My husband and I had decided to sell our house and be closer to his aging parents. We wanted to be far enough that she would need to plan to see them. We wanted her to work on herself for once. All alone. She would have to pull herself from hell and learn to lean into God for guidance, just like I had. So, we announced to my family that we were going to sell. My sister had given sobriety a new try again. She detoxed at home, but this time had found a new drug program that could easily be maintained remotely, which so many of them don't allow. A program that allowed her to get medication and counseling and stay on track with weekly check-ins. She was to pass a drug test in order to get the medication that helped her not have detox symptoms. The nerve pain, sweats, nausea and more could be contained if she stayed in this program. The one thing that sent her back to using drugs every time stressful life situations and the fear of the detox symptoms.

That Winter, we sold our home and I invited my mom to come to live with us. My mom was still a single widow. She needed a break from dealing with my sister. It weighed on her heavily mentally. She sold her home and told Cameron she would need to find somewhere else to live. I could tell she wanted me to invite my sister to join in the move, but that was absolutely not happening. Finding a temporary place to live would seem scary and overwhelming and we knew she had no money and no job, but she had sobriety and she would have to find her strength right now. Was it too much to push on her? Possibly so! But, in life… remaining in the white cloud phase for too long, where everything is going smoothly and happily, I think it makes it hard to survive in the real world. Shit happens. Hard shit happens to all of us. So, you have to find those ways to approach problems head-on and just get over that problem. Ignoring it, dwelling on it, and crying about it never solve it. Working for it and praying for your problems will get you much further in life. You have to realize daily things can happen to throw your mood off if you allow it. You have to be bigger mentally than that problem and focus on blessings, however small they may be. I told her that I was bringing the kids to our new home and that if she wanted to see the kids, I needed to see if she was complying with her drug program and trying to find a job. I told her to reach out to one or two friends who would allow her to possibly stay short-term. I honestly didn't trust anyone around her circle, but she needed to make the decision on who would be the best fit. I also told her if she could find a job close to where we were moving and it could be a fresh start for her. Far away from all the familiar faces that helped her get her drug fix. I explained that we (our mom and I) would help her get set up in temporary housing till she could save to get her own place once she had a job nearby us.

At that point, I would consider letting her kids move back in with her. She knew that I could go to the courthouse and file for emergency custody easily. I had proof that she and her children's father weren't fit to be parents at that time. She had no ground to stand on to argue back. When I knew she had maintained sobriety, had held a job and was able to handle life, I would want the kids to come live with her. This gave her goals to work for. Obtainable goals. Being without the distraction of the kids allowed her to dig deep mentally, and she only had her inner demons to battle in the silence.

Now, it was do or die. We moved the kids' mid-school year during Christmas break. I wouldn't advise ever selling and buying a home during this time of the year! Talk about added stress! But we managed somehow to make it through closing dates changing, more money being paid out for this or that and finally, a horribly stormy moving day. I enrolled my niece and nephew in gymnastics and ninja to allow them something to do that helped take the focus off their mom and dad not being around. They face-timed Cameron daily. Occasionally they spoke to their dad. Cameron was living and staying on the couch of a guy friend in a really small apartment. She was not happy about the arrangements but was thankful not to be homeless. She was raring to get closer to us, so she could see the kids and be a part of their lives again. I stayed true to my word and told her she couldn't come until she had a job lined up. After some job interviews were arranged, I told her she could come up for a few days to easier get to job interviews. She came up on a Sunday. The kids were thrilled to get to spend time with her. I know despite how much of a stable and happy environment I created for them, the worry and trauma they had experienced were still inside them. I was happy to see she had maintained sobriety when she came inside. She looked happier, but I could tell being away from the kids this time really weighed on her. I decided that year to really begin finding ways to encourage them without harping on her past, maintain my boundaries of trust for myself with her and set more of a positive example for her. The idea for this book came during that time. I knew we had an incredible story to tell the world. But I also think without patience, it wasn't time just yet. The story was still being written.

Chapter 16: Look What You Can Do!

Going through a viral epidemic while also maintaining sobriety must have been so incredibly difficult for my sister. The world was like nothing any of us had ever seen. People were wearing masks, schools were shut down and cases of the virus were on the rise. The government was shutting down businesses. The impact was felt by everyone. I felt it, so I know she felt it more. I had my ways to deal with, but would my sister? When she went back to her friend's apartment again after the job interviews, she was becoming depressed with no job offerings. That's when I told her to come back for two days, and we would hit the concrete, dropping off resumes the old-school way. I wanted her to see that hard work would pay off. That stopping just because you weren't getting instant gratification from your efforts was why you would stop growing as a person. I was learning this too. I'd given so many business opportunities a go and not finished them when they began to fail in my eyes. If it got too hard, I gave up. I wanted them to be successful, but was I doing the right things to get myself to where I wanted to be? Self-reflection is a hard thing for most humans to go through. To really find the things that need work within ourselves, acknowledge and change, and find ways to better yourself. I was determined myself, and I needed her to be too. Maybe it was me turning thirty-nine this year, or maybe I was just tired of being let down myself, so I made changes. I focused on the things that made me happy. I worked late and put more effort into the goals I wanted to accomplish. I hoped my sister was taking notice. I know the children in my life were noticing that both my sister and I were working hard to better ourselves. They were thriving in school. Thriving in extracurriculars. Lead by example, people! GOSH! This is so needed in the current world of social media. Don't say that my kids don't listen, when you are not listening to what you know it takes to get the job done either! EEK, did I just strike a nerve? Yaa, I'm calling most people out, including myself. Because we harp on our kids and people who aren't where they are capable of being it's judgment, especially when we ourselves aren't usually on a golden pedestal. We all have made and will make mistakes in life. The true lesson is learning from that mistake and trying to do better.

My sister came again and we spent nearly two days driving around every place we could find. I could see the determination on her face, but her spirit was becoming weak. I kept encouraging her to stay hopeful and keep her light on it. Don't let off the gas yet! That's when the breakthroughs begin to happen. When you get past the hard disappointments, that's when you're often rewarded. Later that day, we were leaving lunch and one of the interviewees called her and gave her that chance she had been waiting on. A chance to prove herself. She started the job that February. My mom and I set her up in an Airbnb home ten minutes away. She had thirty days to save every little bit of money to put down as a deposit somewhere from working this new job. She focused on work, seeing the kids on the weekends, and saving. She put the work in, and that paid off. She was able to find a townhome for rent nine minutes from my new house. She would have to drive to work, but it would allow me to be able to help with getting kids to school and from school. My mom would be able to help, too and she had a good support system. She moved in March and was so happy! She was exhausted but had been sober for several months at this point. She was able to have that quiet self-reflection without distractions for thirty days and now she had her own place. It's amazing what can happen in a year, both good and bad. You can make so much progress if you stick to your goals, say no to things that don't serve you, and put God and your family first. When you least expect it, the blessings start to flow in. When you start living a healthier and balanced life, the right things will come to you. Your energy will shift, and it will shift in the world around you. The people you attract change. That spring, my sister began talking to a new guy. She was immediately smitten, but I reminded her not to lose focus. I honestly thought it was too soon. However, when I met him a few months after they started dating, I knew what she saw in him. He was younger but had a good heart filled with positivity. He was joyful, encouraging, hardworking, and fit right into our family. He reminded me a lot of our dad, and I knew this was God's work. I knew my dad had hand-picked him and placed him in that exact location for them to be able to meet. Both living hours from their own hometowns. Early on, I learned he also had been through recovery, but he had done inpatient treatment where he lived onsite at a men's recovery. At first, I thought this was a disaster waiting to happen. No matter how much I adored him as a person, that worry of one of them failing would always be there. Trust would take time. As time passed, he spent a lot of time at my home. He continued to live in his recovery location. We would go to as a family to church on Sundays and it gave me a chance to get to know who he really was. I wasn't wrong in my initial observation. He was all of those things. He was also exactly what my sister needed. He was at the front of the train, and she was following in his footsteps of sobriety and wanting to find healthy ways to deal with stress. The kids took a liking to him as well, which was the best blessing. He made it known and told us often that he understood they were a package deal. He never wanted to fill their dads' shoes, but he would be a stable man they could depend on. After all the kids had gone through, I couldn't help but be so thankful. He was quickly becoming someone I respected. He was honest about his past from the first day I met him, all of it, and to me, that showed he was a changed person. So, I trusted slowly but surely. My sister was continuing to work and maintain sobriety, and I knew what the next step was in this journey. Forgiveness!

Chapter 17: Surprise

I found out today that my sister's boyfriend is asking her to marry him. I cried, jumped for joy, and relished in the excitement of being. He let me help plan the engagement, and I couldn't be more thrilled for her life to continue to go in the right direction. No one knows yet, except me, my mom, and him. Next weekend he will get down on one knee under the Christmas lights of an enchanted location and do a storybook engagement written in the stars. I will get to witness my sister heal in ways I could only dream about one day. To receive the love she always wished for. To have a man choose her to grow old with. Yes, I'm crying happy tears as I type this. I never ever thought I would see this day come. I thought by now my sister would be in the ground, so to be here now is almost like a dream. They also just told us that they are expecting a BABY! What a blessing, a real-life blessing! In the next few weeks, we will find out the sex of the baby, but for now, I just get to relish in all the excitement that's coming her way and our way! The blessings are flowing, and I do not forget to thank God every night before my head hits that pillow to sleep. I honestly don't know if I've taken a proper deep breath in years. I'm able to breathe now. I know my sister will continue to put in the work necessary to remain sober. I know that her boyfriend will do the same. Together, they are defying the odds stacked against them. He told me recently that in one of his support groups when he first began, they told him that out of about twenty men who sat there that night, they informed them that several would be homeless and using again and that a couple of them would be dead the coming year.

As they sat in that room, I could only imagine the impact that day had. He told me that this statement was life-changing. He didn't want to be one of the statistics. He himself had come from a family who abused drugs. He was literally born into it. He admitted that if he had never gotten into trouble that sent him to rehab, he would have still been an addict. But you know what I find honorable in him? He didn't just stay the one year he was given in rehab. He asked to remain for another year to continue to focus on his sobriety. He didn't take the easy way out. He put the work in. That example is something my sister I know has learned from. I'll be honored to call him family.

Chapter 18: Forgiving Is How You Heal

I wanted to forgive my sister for all she had put us through with her addiction. But saying it and doing the work takes two very different mindsets. I couldn't simply just forget it, just because she was doing well now. Lord knows she had pulled the safety rug out from under us before. So, how do you trust someone who has broken your trust so many times? You did it with a lot of patience and no expectations. I couldn't simply expect anything from Cameron. With time, I had to just watch and wait and let the trust build naturally. She knew this as I had told her I couldn't just let that worry go that she would fall back into her old life. However, time sometimes does break down the walls of trust with action. She and I spent a lot of time talking, really talking about our feelings. So many things we had brushed under the rug. The hurtful, the emotional, the happy, the funny things. We shared our lives. For many things, we had not been there for each other, and learning about each other I think it gave us a new understanding of the choices we made. I was beginning to forgive the hurt. After all, it's a true statement that holding onto resentment only hurts you inside. It affects you mentally and physically more than it does the other person who hurt you. I couldn't dwell on that resentment of all her addiction stole from me. I had to learn to live in the present, not the past. We made goals for our future. We took our first family vacation in many years together and made good memories! I continued to work on my healing through meditation, yoga, exercise, writing, spending time with good friends and even my marriage. I had abandoned my marriage during the chaos. It was time to put in the hard work to get it where it should be. I had little eyes watching, and they needed to know and understand what marriage is and what it means to give to someone else selflessly.

For the last, almost twenty years, nearly half my life has been hard. The next twenty years were going to be memorable. I was going to win. I was going to put the work into my projects, myself, my marriage, my children and I was going to freaking win. Failure wasn't an option. My sister taught me that. Despite the horrible things we went through, we never gave up hope that it would get better. So, every Christmas, when you see my house decorated with too many trees lit, a buffet of food on our table, and smiling happy kids and adults creating last memories, know that it didn't come without sacrifice in more ways than one. We celebrate Christmas for a reason for the season, Jesus. We celebrate because we have a chance now to be a family, despite the hardships we've faced. We celebrate because that Christmas morning that traumatized us as kids will not win. My dad's spirit is at peace, and so are we.

www.ingramcontent.com/pod-product-compliance
Lightning Source LLC
Chambersburg PA
CBHW061038050726

47592CB00004B/1499